First Penance

The Sacrament of Reconciliation

PREPARING

CELEBRATING

REMEMBERING

Text by
FRANCES C. HEEREY, S.C.H.

Illustrations by
RITA GOODWILL

D0522851

Nihil Obstat: Rev. Msgr. John A. Alesandro, S.T.L., J.C.D.

Imprimatur: Most Rev. John R. McGann, D.D.
Bishop of Rockville Centre
July 2, 1984

PRINTED IN BELGIUM

NAME _Giulio Ian Thuburn_

I was born on _13th June 1980_

I was Baptized on _21st June_

I received my First Penance on

Happy the merciful: they shall have mercy shown them.

MATTHEW 5:7

Table of Contents

Preface

Dear Children and Parents,

We are made in the image and likeness of God. At our Baptism God the Father, God the Son, and God the Holy Spirit came into our souls and gave us new life in God. God is a God of love and mercy. As God's children then, we try to show love and mercy to everyone.

To teach us the way to live good lives God the Father sent His Son Jesus to be with us, as a child and as a man. When He was a child, Jesus went to school. He studied the Scriptures. He learned that God gave Moses the 10 Commandments. If people followed the 10 Commandments they would be happy. Jesus learned his lessons well. When Jesus was a man, He taught about the kingdom of God. He told stories of mercy, forgiveness, and happiness. He taught us how to pray. Some of Jesus' teachings are in this book.

This text is designed to help the young learn

what it means to be children of God and followers of Jesus. It can be used to prepare children for the first reception of the Sacrament of Penance. It can be a means to remember what Jesus taught each time children go to confession. It is intended to teach happiness with Jesus.

As children settle into the arms of our God as lambs in the arms of a shepherd, they will know the beautiful meaning of Jesus' words:

If anyone loves me he will keep my word, and my Father will love him, and we shall come to him and make our home in him.

JOHN 14:23

I AM GOOD

I am good because God made me. God is a God of mercy and a God of love. God our Father made me in His image and likeness.

> Jesus is the Son of God.
> The Holy Spirit is the Spirit of Jesus and God the Father.
> The Holy Spirit gives me the power to live as a child of God.

As a child of God I try to love God and everyone that God has made: my parents, my guardians, my brothers and sisters, my friends, the unborn, the handicapped, the elderly, people who are in need of my love.

Jesus wants me to follow Him in His love and mercy. I'll often think of some of the wonderful things Jesus said and did. When I follow Jesus, I am unselfish.

I act as a loving child of God when I obey Jesus' law of love, the 10 Commandments of God, and the Commandments of the Church, and when I show mercy and forgiveness.

CELEBRATING

The Mercy of God

Oh how I need you, Jesus.
My heart is bursting with desire for You.
You teach me what's right.
You make my life bright.
Forever You are my BEST FRIEND.

Oh how I praise You, Jesus.
My heart is bursting with praise for You.
You show me the way
To serve You each day.
Forever You give me Your SPIRIT.

Oh how I thank you, Jesus.
My heart is bursting with gratitude.
You forgive me my wrongs.
You forgive me my sins.
Forever You show me Your MERCY.

Amen.   Alleluia.

REMEMBERING

1. **Why am I good?**

   I am good because God who is goodness made me.

2. **Who is Jesus?**

   Jesus is the Son of God our Father. He is both God and Man.

3. **Who is the Holy Spirit?**

   The Holy Spirit is the spirit of Jesus and God the Father.

4. **What does the Holy Spirit do?**

   The Holy Spirit gives me power to live as a child of God.

5. **How can I live as a child of God?**

   I live as a child of God when I love God and everyone that He has made, when I obey His commandments, and when I show mercy and forgiveness to others.

6. Who are the people I must love?

I must love my parents, my guardians, my brothers and sisters, my friends, the unborn, the handicapped, the elderly, people who are in need of my love.

7. What are the commandments I must obey?

I must obey the 10 Commandments of God and the Commandments of the Church.

JESUS

These are some of the things Jesus did to show how much He loves us and forgives us.

Jesus was born in Bethlehem. His mother was Mary, His foster father was Joseph. We celebrate Jesus' Birthday on Christmas Day.

He studied the scripture and learned from good teachers.

Jesus was kind to everybody.

Jesus suffered and died to gain forgiveness for all our sins.

ALLELUIA

Jesus' life and death show us the mercy of God.

He was raised from the dead. Amen. Alleluia.

He returned to His Father in Heaven.

He sent us the Holy Spirit to give us power to follow Him.

I will always trust in the mercy of Jesus. Amen.   Alleluia.

SERMON ON THE MOUNT

PREPARING

When you go to Mass or a prayer service, the priest usually gives a homily. Another name for homily is sermon. In his homily the priest tells you special stories to help you understand all about Jesus' love.

Jesus also gave homilies. A famous homily is the Sermon on the Mount or the Eight Beatitudes. Jesus told His followers about real happiness and the Kingdom of God. Let us listen to Jesus' words.

1. How happy are the poor in spirit:
   theirs is the kingdom of heaven.

2. Happy the gentle:
   they shall have the earth for their heritage.

3. Happy those who mourn:
   they shall be comforted.

4. Happy those who hunger and thirst for
      what is right:
   they shall be satisfied.

5. Happy the MERCIFUL:
   they shall have mercy shown them.

6. Happy the pure in heart:
   they shall see God.

7. Happy the peacemakers:
   they shall be called the children of God.

8. Happy those who are persecuted in the
      cause of right:
   theirs is the kingdom of heaven.

Jesus also said,

*I have not come to do away with the Law of Moses
and the teachings of the prophets, but to make their
teachings come true.*

MATTHEW 5:17

CELEBRATING

Sometimes we play "Happiness Is" games in school or at parties. This is a Happiness song based on the Eight Beatitudes or Jesus' sermon. See if you can make up a melody to go with this song.

Happiness is:

1. Knowing God is near me.

2. Being gentle in spirit.

3. Helping others feel better.

4. Trying to do what is right.

5. Being merciful and forgiving.

6. Looking and listening for God.

7. Bringing peace to others.

8. Knowing God loves me.

Amen.   Alleluia.

REMEMBERING

1. What is the Sermon on the Mount?

These are the lessons on real happiness which Jesus gave His people. He sat on a hillside and He preached a homily.

2. What do you mean by the word sermon?

Usually during Mass or a prayer service the priest gives us special explanations to help us understand better the words that Jesus spoke.

3. What is another name for the Sermon on the Mount?

Another name for the Sermon on the Mount is the Eight BEATITUDES.

JUSTICE AND PEACE

If we remember to do the following acts, we shall truly live the Sermon on the Mount. We shall have happiness. We shall bring peace and reconciliation wherever we go.

Help the elderly.

Take care of babies.

Provide shelter and food for other people.

Forgive people who hurt you. Comfort those who cry.

Express love by trying to change things that are harmful to other people.

Assist God our Father to help all people who are in need.

THE PRODIGAL SON

The Prodigal Son

This is a favorite story of Catholic girls and boys. Jesus told the story to show how much God loves us, even when we do wrong things. Think about this story often. It will tell you many things about God's love and mercy.

Once upon a time a son took all his belongings and ran away from his father's house.

When he had spent all his money, he had no food. He lost all his friends. He was so lonely and frightened. He said to himself, ''I must go back to my father's house. I am so sorry I did wrong.''

Every day the boy's father stood waiting for his son to come home. He loved him so much. He really missed him.

One day the father saw his son coming up the road. He ran with arms outstretched to greet his son. The son was so happy. He knew he was loved and forgiven. His father had mercy.

The father hugged his son. The boy said, ''I

am sorry, Father. I did a foolish thing. I did not obey your law of love. I was wrong." He was so happy to be back in his father's home. He promised never to do wrong again.

Amen.   Alleluia!

Jesus told the story to teach us about God's love, mercy, forgiveness, sin.

1. This is what SIN is:

It is to disobey God's law of love deliberately.

2. This is what God's LOVE is:

It is patiently waiting for us to come home to Him.

3. This is what God's MERCY is:

It is to be kind and forgiving when we do wrong.

4. This is what God's FORGIVENESS is:

It is to wait patiently. It is to reach out to the person who hurt us. It is to forget the hurt.

LORD JESUS,
SON OF GOD,
HAVE MERCY ON ME A SINNER.

COMMANDMENTS

The Ten Commandments of God

Moses was a faithful prophet and a leader of God's people. He lived many years before Jesus was born. God gave Moses ten directions to help his people live good lives. Jesus obeyed these directions. They are called the Ten Commandments of God.

THE TEN COMMANDMENTS OF GOD

1. I, the Lord, am your God. You shall not have strange gods besides me.
2. You shall not take the name of the Lord God in vain.
3. Remember to keep holy the Sabbath.
4. Honor your father and mother.
5. You shall not kill.
6. You shall not commit adultery.
7. You shall not steal.

8. You shall not bear false witness against your neighbor.

9. You shall not covet your neighbor's wife.

10. You shall not covet your neighbor's goods.

Jesus' Commandment of Love

MATTHEW 22:37-40

''You must love the Lord your God with all your heart, with all your soul, and with all your mind. This is the greatest and the first commandment. The second resembles it: You must love your neighbor as yourself. On these two commandments depend the whole law, and the prophets also.''

Commandments of the Church

To help us follow God's laws of love (the 10 Commandments), the Church gives us simple rules to follow. They are called the Commandments of the Church.

COMMANDMENTS OF THE CHURCH

1. To keep holy the day of the Lord's resurrection.
2. To receive Holy Communion frequently and the Sacrament of Reconciliation regularly.
3. To study Catholic teaching.
4. To observe the marriage laws of the Church.
5. To strengthen and support the Church.
6. To do penance.
7. To join in the missionary spirit of the Church.

RITE OF THE SACRAMENT

PREPARING

Occasionally we find ourselves doing or thinking things that are hurtful to other people and to ourselves. Sometimes we do not do the things for others or ourselves that we are responsible for. When we do, think, or omit things on purpose, we disobey God's law of love. This is called sin. By sin we hurt others and ourselves.

How can we make up to God and to others? We can do that by being sorry and telling that to God and to others. We can tell God in the Sacrament of Penance. We must remember the most important lesson learned: *God loves us very much!* He forgives us when we confess our sins to Him.

At Confession we are welcomed back and we share PEACE with God and one another.

CELEBRATING

This is the way we celebrate the Sacrament of Penance or Reconciliation, (in 5 steps).

BEFORE CONFESSION
1. We *think* of our sins, with Jesus.
2. We are *sorry* for our sins.
3. We *decide* not to sin again.

IN CONFESSION

The priest welcomes us.
We pray the Sign of the Cross.
The priest talks to us in the name of the Father.
He reads from the scriptures.
4. We *confess* what we did wrong. The priest helps us to do better. We tell God we are sorry. The priest forgives us in the name of God and His people. He gives us a penance. We thank the priest and God.

AFTER CONFESSION
5. We *do our penance*.

A SIMPLE PRAYER

O God, I remember how wonderfully I am
   made.
You made me because you love me.
You made other people because you love
   them.
Sometimes I am not kind
   or I do not care for other people in need.
I know I have hurt them and myself.
I know I have forgotten to love you and them.
I am really sorry.
I need you, Jesus,
   to help me love our Father and other
   people.
I need you, Father,
   to help me follow Jesus in his way of
   love.
I need you, Holy Spirit,
   to help me forgive and love other people
   who hurt me.

Thank you,
   for the gift of this wonderful sacrament
   which gives me the Peace of Jesus.
Amen.

REMEMBERING

1. **What is the Sacrament of Penance?**

   Penance is the sacrament which gives us a special way to show God we are sorry for our sins. It is an action by which God shows His mercy and forgiveness.

2. **What is sin?**

   Sin is disobeying God's law of love deliberately.

3. **What is God's law of love?**

   God's law of love is found in the words of Jesus:

   This is the first:

   Hear, O Israel! The Lord our God is Lord alone! Therefore, you shall love the Lord your God with all your heart
   with all your soul
   with all your mind
   with all your strength.

   This is the second:

   You shall love your neighbor as yourself.

   MARK 12:28

4. What are the other Commandments which God has given us?

God has given us the Ten Commandments.

5. What is Confession?

Confession is telling God that we have done certain sins and that we are sorry.

6. How does the Church bring God's forgiveness in confession?

The Church brings God's forgiveness in confession through the priest.

7. What are the special steps we take in going to confession?

1. We think of our sins.
2. We are sorry for our sins.
3. We decide not to sin again.
4. We confess what we did.
5. We do our penance.

8. What do we mean by "We do our penance?"

We say the prayers or do the activity that the priest gives us immediately after our confession.

EXAMINATION OF CONSCIENCE

BEFORE CONFESSION

Some helps for me to remember my sins.

A. *I pray:* God our Father, I trust in your mercy and forgiveness. I remember that you made me, I know that you love me. I want to follow your Son Jesus in His goodness always. I ask you to help me to see how I hurt others and myself. I ask you to help me to see where I have offended you. Help me to do better.

B. *I will read the story of the Prodigal Son.*

C. *I will think about the Commandments of God like this:*

1. Have I remembered to tell God every day how much I love and need Him?

2. Have I remembered always to speak Jesus' name in a holy way?

3. Have I worshipped God by going to Mass on Sunday?

4. Have I tried to obey my parents and other people who take care of me?

5. Have I remembered to
help the elderly   act justly
avoid fighting   take care of babies
care for people   forgive people
   in need   who hurt me
give food to the hungry.

6. Have I failed to respect myself and other people, and to realize that our bodies are God's special creations?

7. Did I take money, toys, bikes, or other things that I didn't own?

8. Have I remembered to say only good things about people. Have I told lies about people?

9. Have I been kind to my neighbor?

10. Have I tried not to be jealous when other people have things I would like to have?

D. *I plan my confession.*

1. I remember how long it has been since I went to confession (one week, two weeks, the FIRST TIME?).

2. I think about how many times I did the wrong things.

3. Without fears, I will tell the priest my sins and that I am sorry for them.

4. I will listen to the priest if he asks me questions. I know that, like Jesus, he loves me.

5. I will ask him questions, if I need to.

6. I will listen for the penance. I will remember it.

7. I will receive the priest's absolution. I know that the absolution is a sign that Jesus forgives me with His merciful love. It is just like the father hugging his prodigal son!

8. I will thank the priest.

9. I will say or do my penance.

AFTER CONFESSION

1. I do or say my penance.
2. I praise God for the wonderful love and mercy shown to me.

PENANCE HELPS US GROW IN GRACE AND HOLINESS.

STATIONS OF THE CROSS

Stations of the Cross

This is a prayer said during Lent. Many people say it all year round. There are fourteen stations.

Prayer

Jesus, I want to be sorry for my sins. Help me to see how you suffered and died for me. Help me to know your mercy and forgiveness. Teach me how to say "Thank You."

+

1. JESUS IS CONDEMNED TO DIE

I am sorry, Jesus.

+

2. JESUS CARRIES HIS CROSS

It looks so heavy, Jesus.

+

3. JESUS FALLS THE FIRST TIME

Your strength is starting to fail.

+

4. JESUS MEETS HIS MOTHER MARY

How sad your Mother felt, Jesus.

+

5. SIMON HELPS JESUS

I must help others who carry heavy loads.

+

6. VERONICA WIPES JESUS' FACE

Teach me to help others in need.

+

7. JESUS FALLS A SECOND TIME

Dear Jesus, how weak you are.

+

8. JESUS MEETS THE WOMEN

Jesus you're so brave. You tell them not to cry.

+

9. JESUS FALLS THE THIRD TIME

Dear Jesus, you are suffering so much.

+

10. JESUS IS STRIPPED OF HIS CLOTHES

How shamefully you were treated.

+

11. JESUS IS NAILED TO THE CROSS

How cruel the people were. I love you.

+

12. JESUS DIES

I know you forgive me my sins.

+

13. JESUS IS TAKEN DOWN
I thank the people who took care of
your body.

+

14. JESUS IS LAID IN THE TOMB
Thank you for your mercy.

After we make the Stations of the Cross, we may wish to speak to Jesus quietly and alone. In addition to our own words and thoughts, we may say these prayers.

ACT OF FAITH

O my God, I believe that you are one God in three Divine Persons: Father, Son and Holy Spirit. I believe that Your Divine Son became Man and died for our sins, and that He will come again to judge the living and the dead. I believe these and all the truths that the Catholic Church teaches, because You have revealed them, who can neither deceive nor be deceived.   Amen.

ACT OF HOPE

O my God, relying on Your almighty power and infinite mercy and promises, I hope to obtain pardon of my sins, the help of Your grace and life everlasting through the merits of Jesus Christ, my Lord and Redeemer. Amen.

ACT OF LOVE

O my God, I love you above all things with my whole heart and soul, because You are all good and worthy of all my love. I love my neighbor as myself for the love of You. I forgive all who have injured me and ask pardon of all whom I have injured.   Amen.

LENT

Lent is a time of preparation to celebrate the death and resurrection of Jesus. We do penance for our sins and tell Jesus and each other ''I am sorry, please forgive me.''

Jesus forgives us through His suffering and death on the cross.

During Lent we get ready for the new life and joy of Easter.

PRAYER

PRAYER

Don't you like talking and listening to friends? Prayer is something like that. Prayer is talking to God. Prayer is listening to God. Prayer is just being with God.

Sometimes we pray alone (in room, in church, anywhere).

Sometimes we pray with others (family, friends, community).

A good way to remember the kinds of prayer we pray is to think of the word ACTS.

They stand for: ADORATION,
CONTRITION,
THANKSGIVING,
SUPPLICATION.

A	Adoration—	I adore you God, Father, Son, Holy Spirit.
C	Contrition—	I confess my sins with real *sorrow*.
T	Thanksgiving—	I thank you, God, for all your wonderful gifts.
S	Supplication—	I ask you for special help for myself and others.

Special Prayers
That We Should Know

THE OUR FATHER

Our Father who art in heaven, hallowed be thy name. Thy kingdom come. Thy will be done on earth as it is in heaven. Give us this day our daily bread and forgive us our trespasses as we forgive those who trespass against us and lead us not into temptation, but deliver us from evil.   Amen.

THE HAIL MARY

Hail Mary full of grace the Lord is with Thee. Blessed art thou among women and blessed is the fruit of thy womb Jesus. Holy Mary Mother of God pray for us sinners now and at the hour of our death.   Amen.

GLORY BE TO THE FATHER

Glory be to the Father and to the Son and to the Holy Spirit, as it was in the beginning is now and ever shall be world without end. Amen.

AN ACT OF CONTRITION

O my God I am heartily sorry for having offended Thee and I detest all my sins because of Thy just punishment, but most of all because they offend Thee, my God, Who are all good, and deserving of all my love. I firmly resolve with the help of Thy grace, to sin no more, and to avoid the near occasions of sin. Amen.

THE APOSTLES CREED

I believe in God, the Father Almighty, Creator of heaven and earth; and in Jesus Christ, His only Son, our Lord; who was conceived by the Holy Spirit, born of the Virgin Mary, suffered under Pontius Pilate, was crucified, died and was buried.

He descended into hell; the third day He arose again from the dead. He ascended into heaven, sits at the right hand of God, the Father Almighty; thence He shall come to judge the living and the dead. I believe in the Holy Spirit, the Holy Catholic Church, the communion of saints, the forgiveness of sins, the resurrection of the body and life everlasting. Amen.

BLESSING BEFORE MEALS

Bless us, Lord, and these Thy gifts which we are about to receive from Thy bountiful hands, through Christ our Lord.   Amen.

GRACE AFTER MEALS

We give Thee thanks, Almighty God, for these Thy gifts through Christ our Lord. Amen.

THE "MEMORARE"

Remember, O most gracious Virgin Mary, that never was it known that anyone who fled to your protection, implored your help or sought your intercession, was left unaided. Inspired with this confidence, I fly to you, O Virgin of virgins, my Mother; to you do I come, before you I stand, sinful and sorrowful. O Mother of the Word Incarnate, despise not my petitions, but in your mercy hear and answer me.   Amen.

THE ROSARY

The rosary is a special way of praying to God that honors Mary, the Mother of Jesus. While reciting prayers, you think about certain stories in the lives of Jesus and Mary. These stories are called mysteries: a mystery is a story about God.

Rosary beads are used to keep count of the prayers and mysteries. Recite the Apostles' Creed while you hold the crucifix, then one Our Father and three Hail Marys. After that, as you think about each mystery, recite the Our Father on the large bead, the Hail Mary on each of ten smaller beads and finish with a Glory Be. That makes one decade. The complete rosary consists of five decades. There are three sets of mysteries and five stories in each set.

The Joyful Mysteries

1. The Coming of Jesus is Announced
2. Mary Visits Elizabeth
3. Jesus is Born
4. Jesus is Presented to God
5. Jesus is Found in the Temple

The Sorrowful Mysteries

1. Jesus' Agony in the Garden
2. Jesus is Whipped
3. Jesus is Crowned with Thorns
4. Jesus Carries His Cross
5. Jesus Dies on the Cross

The Glorious Mysteries

1. Jesus Rises from His Tomb
2. Jesus Ascends to Heaven
3. The Holy Spirit Descends
4. Mary is Assumed into Heaven
5. Mary is Crowned in Heaven

PRAYER TO THE HOLY SPIRIT

Come, O Holy Spirit, fill the hearts of Your faithful and kindle in them the fire of Your love.

V. Send forth Your Spirit and they shall be created.

R. And You shall renew the face of the earth.

Let us pray:

O God, who has taught the hearts of the faithful by the light of the Holy Spirit, grant that in the same Spirit, we may be always truly wise and ever rejoice in His consolation. Through Christ our Lord. Amen.

SHORT PRAYERS

Dear God, I love you with all my heart and soul. You are all good and I shall never stop loving You. Teach me to love you more each day.

Dear God, I am sorry for all my sins. Help me never to commit them any more.

Jesus, have mercy on the poor souls in purgatory. Help them come to You.

REWARD

He will come again in glory to judge the living and the dead, and his kingdom will have no end.

PROFESSION OF FAITH

Every boy and girl likes a reward. In His great love Jesus will reward us for being good to others. Jesus said to do these things:

> feed hungry people
> give drink to thirsty people
> give clothes to the needy
> take care of the sick
> visit people in prison

Our reward? Jesus says:

> Come, you that are blessed by my Father,
> Come and possess the kingdom which has been prepared for you since the creation of the world.

To live with Jesus forever and ever! Isn't that a happy hope!

Amen.   Alleluia.

Outstanding
CHILDREN'S BOOKS

Available from your local dealer or religious book store.